Con

Body Language Explained:

How to Master the Power of the

Unconscious

By C.K. Murray

Body language is *everything*.

Every minute of every day, our bodies are talking. When we're finishing that last bit of work, when we're walking around our neighborhoods, moving about our grocery stores, at sporting events and movie theatres and shopping malls and stores and interacting with a cashier at the drive-thru at McDonald's—everywhere we go, our bodies speak. From the way we tilt our heads, blink our eyes, touch our noses and move our mouths; everything we don't say, says something.

In fact, studies show that the spoken word only comprises *a fraction* of total communication. The words that come from our mouths are only 7% of what we say. 55% is through body language, and the other 38% comes through tone and speed of voice.

Body language is the single most innate form of human communication, and most of us never take the time to consider it.

Like nearly all of our basic, mammalian functions, body language originates in the limbic system. The basic role of the limbic system is to keep us alive and reproductive, and it is through body language that this happens. Infant crying indicates that babies need food, water, and protection. Arched eyebrows, full lips, and erogenous contact indicate sexual arousal; mechanisms for survival and pleasure— ways to communicate when words fall short.

In short, body language is the reason we continue to live. It is an indicator of our needs and wants, even a direct display of the relative health of our minds and bodies. And though we may consider it a phenomenon largely unconscious, it is well within our conscious power. What we fail to realize is incredible. If we can learn to *control* our body language and *capitalize* on the power of nonverbal communication, then we can learn to *command* our lives for the better.

No matter your position or trajectory in life, whether you're a part-time worker, a careerist, or currently unemployed—understanding body language is essential. By communicating the right signals to the right people, we literally dictate what they think and how they react. And when these everyday behavioral responses change, everything else is gravy.

Think about it.

If you want to show others that you are a powerful, confident individual, are you going to walk around with your shoulders hunched and your head low, *or* are you going to keep your back straight, your head high, and your fearless eyes focused to the task? Do you want to gain respect and admiration from those around you? Do you want to sink into obscurity like everybody else or do you want to *be* somebody?

The choice is yours, because frankly, body language is yours. By consciously adopting the right body signals, movements and positions, we can maximize our opportunities for success. Whether that be success in the workplace, in the public sphere, in private matters—you name it. Throughout conscious application of body language, we become masters of the *un*conscious. And by making the right body language *un*conscious, we can influence others without them ever even knowing.

Sound devious?

Maybe a little, but that's only because humans are such instinctual creatures. See, body language is all about science. It's all about taking what has been proven to work, and enacting it in everyday situations. Through enough practice, and the right attitude, body language can transform our lives.

Still skeptical? Well you should be, body language is a lot more complex than you ever thought…

Know Your Body: Why the Language You Speak is Rarely Spoken

You've probably heard of body language to some extent or another. In cases of attraction, we've all heard the typical signs. In women, a hair flip may indicate sexual interest, and in men, puffing out his chest may indicate an attempt to look 'macho.'

Depending upon the context, body language can serve a variety of functions. Handshakes are used in the business world to solidify trust and reciprocation. Nods may indicate agreement, whereas frowns or head-shaking may indicate disagreement. To some, a smile shows interest; however, a smile that does not extend to the eyes and does not create crow's feet, may very well be artificial.

When it comes to body language, it's all about what to display and what to look for. So if we're going to master the art of the wordless whisper or speechless shout, we've got to learn the most important part: the body!

For now, let's cover the basics before delving into the more advanced:

The Eyes

They say the eyes are the window to the soul, and this is very well true. A few things to keep in mind when evaluating another's eyes is the gaze itself, the rate of blinking, and the pupil size. A prolonged gaze that is direct will typically indicate interest and attention, whereas eyes that break contact may indicate disinterest, discomfort, or concealment. People who look for very long could very well be faking interest, and people who look away may simply be distracted by something else. There is not always an ulterior motive, but generally strong eye contact is a good sign, and weak contact indicates that other things are more pressing to the person.

Another thing to consider is blinking. Frequent blinking typically means discomfort or stress. It could also mean something is in the person's eye! Lack of blinking, on the other hand, may indicate a conscious effort to control the eyes. This, in and of itself, hints at a degree of deception if not secrecy. Again, these are basic assumptions that can be made. To get a better idea of the individual's behaviors and why, contextual clues should be considered. Are there allergens in the air? Is the lighting harsh? Does the person seem tired or energetic—perhaps from lack of sleep, or perhaps energetic from something consumed?

A better, more physiologically-based way to assess individual eyes comes from the pupils. Pupil size will change depending upon nearby light. Small pupils indicate more light, big ones indicate lack of light. However, pupils also indicate other important beliefs or feelings. Pupils will increase in size when the person likes what he or she sees. This means an attraction, whether physical or sexual or simply to something that has occurred or been said. Smaller pupils may indicate the opposite. Furthermore, noticeably small pupils—"pinheads"—can indicate drug use of painkillers and heroin. Big pupils may indicate cocaine, ecstasy, and hallucinogen use.

The Mouth

This is another part of the body that reveals a lot about what we're thinking. The biggest one, obviously, is the smile. Smiles can be genuine or they can fake happiness, sarcasm and a variety of emotions. Genuine smiles are sometimes hard to read but can be determined if we know what to look for. Basically, a genuine smile involves two muscle groups and an inauthentic smile does not. Called the Duchenne smile, a genuine smile raises the corners of the mouth and also raises the cheeks and forms crow's feet around the eyes. Fake smiles do not raise the cheeks nor do they form crow's feet around the eyes in such fashion.

Of course, many experts argue that even a 'genuine' smile can be faked. Further research is required to tease apart the reals from the phonies—assuming we're dealing with a deceptive master of smiles.

The lips are very powerful indicators of body language. Lip biting usually occurs when people are nervous or worried. It can also come with suppressed sexual desire. If the lips are also slightly parted (and licked), then something erotic is *definitely* about to go down! Of course, parted lips may simply mean that a person is about to talk.

Lip pursing typically comes with feelings of frustration—when pulled inward all around. However, it can also indicate anger and lying. The pursing motion itself represents the body's last ditch effort to keep from saying something controversial. Of course, the pursing can also simply represent indecision, as a person decides between various opinions or options.

In romance, puckered lips forming a kiss shape indicate desire. In fact, the lips are often displayed in this fashion to accentuate their plumpness—a known sexual turn-on.

When the lips are turned in or 'swallowed' they usually indicate secretive knowledge, disapproval, or thought. If a person is trying to hide true emotions, he or she will cover the mouth. Slight deviations such as upturns or downturns in the lips can indicate happiness or sadness, respectively.

Basically, the lips are complex organs. They indicate a whole range of emotions and thoughts—and sometimes downright confuse us. Without taking into account the situation and other body language signs, the lips may be more than we can handle. Which is why we need to continue reading…

The Appendages

This refers to the arms, legs, hands and feet. If you're ever in a public space and you notice somebody looking at you with a certain gaze of attraction, you might also notice something else: leg and foot position. People will typically point their toes toward the object of attraction, even if their bodies are facing elsewhere. In other words, the foot points and the heart follows. Of course, you should also view the other body signs before concluding too much. Perhaps the person's foot is simply pointing toward an exit from the current conversation. In that case, maybe you just *happen* to be in that line of escape.

We should also make a habit of looking for crossing. Whether the crossing of legs or arms, crossing is typically a bad sign. It indicates disinterest, defensiveness, and self-protection. The person may simply be trying to minimize his or her presence. In many ways, it simply says "leave me alone, I'm not here." Still, we should consider the possibility that maybe it's just cold?

When it comes to the hands, fidgetiness signals nervousness and anxiety. Disinterest or an interest in something else are also indicated, especially when finger-drumming is involved. Hands on the hips may indicate a skepticism or aggression, and hands behind the back can hint at boredom, anger, and a desire to get away. Of course, this isn't always the case. The person may simply find such a pose relaxing, opening the front of the body to advances. In this case, hands clasped behind the back simply show that the individual is willing to interact with others head-on.

There you have it.

You've just learned some of the most basic forms of body language. And if you're anything like me, you might just be very unsatisfied. If so, don't fret. What we have to understand is that body language is a growing science, and that we should *never* assume something about somebody based on just one sign. Instead, we need to seek 'clusters' of body language. If a person's arms and legs show aggression but the eyes show happiness, we need to consider why. We need to think about who the person is, what the situation is, and why that apparent contradiction may exist. In many cases, knowing that person takes time, and over time, we are better able to understand those strange body quirks. Again, we don't understand body language by simply sitting down and reading a dictionary of appearances. And this would be misleading anyway, as certain body language signs change depending upon the culture. So prepare yourself, because what you think you know, you probably don't. And if you ever plan on fitting into a foreign culture, whether on vacation, business, or new residence, you *better* up your body game!

Culture Clash: Body Language Differences Across the World

Imagine this: you're in the biggest business meeting of your life. You've got everything planned, the presentation is ready to go, your proposal is air-tight, and your confidence is booming. As far as you're concerned, everything is on lock-down.

But then it happens. You meet your foreign business partners-to-be and you blow it. Before the actual meeting even begins, you've ruined your chances.

So the question is: what did you do?

Well, if you're like a lot of people, you probably didn't fully adapt to the different culture. See, when it comes to body language, not all of it is universal. While experts contend that facial expressions of sadness, anger, and happiness are generally similar, it is the territory of *the gesture* where things become difficult.

If you make the wrong move and send the wrong signal, you might just ruin your chances. Whether important business meeting, or everyday interaction with a person from a different culture, knowing differences in body language across the world is critical.

Let's take a look at what we should know:

Mind the Eyes

In many cultures, we are taught to make eye contact and hold it. This is a skill developed for everyday interactions, especially when meeting a superior in a formal context. However, what may seem like a respectful and confident gesture in the West, is considered impolite elsewhere. When you look somebody in the eye in such a manner in Asia or Africa, it is typically viewed as a sign of aggression. It means you are challenging the person or attempting to show that you are somehow the superior. Limited eye contact with an individual is actually preferable, indicating respect and deference.

Expressions

The face is our most expressive body part. Although it is used to convey our feelings, emotions, and attitudes, it can also easily deceive. Whether Western or Eastern World, mastering the face is a great way to convey what you want, when you want. In the West, we are taught to express true feelings in order to foster communication and unity. In the East, however—especially in Asia—self-control takes precedence. This means that Asians are expected to be reserved, emotionless even. Showing your cards, so to speak, can be seen as a sign of weakness or promiscuity. Instead, when people in Asia smile, they may simply be indicating something as minor as "yes," "I don't comprehend"—or it may be a cover-up attempt. The smile that we equate to happiness in the West does not necessarily mean the same in the East.

Watch Your Mouth

Obviously, kissing indicates affection, love, romance or lust in the West. People will also use it as a means of greeting and departing. In Asia, kissing in public is not allowed, as it is considered a very intimate act. In Southern Europe, kissing is a standard greeting, even if the other person is not known. In countries such as France and Switzerland, women kiss men and other women, whereas men typically hug other men unless they are related. In Filipino, Native American, Puerto Rican, and certain Latin American cultures, the lips are actually used to point instead of the finger.

Nothing like a little pucker to leave us *totally* confused…

The Nod

Many of us know this as a gesture that indicates agreement or understanding. Unfortunately, in some cultures doing this will only indicate the opposite of what you intend. In parts of Greece, Turkey, Yugoslavia and Bulgaria, for instance, nodding your head actually means that you disagree. Furthermore, many Asian countries discourage head use and touching. Because the spirit is believed to reside in the head, touching another person's head is typically an encroachment of spiritual grounds.

Foot and Legs

In Asia and the Middle East, sitting balanced and solidly is the dominant custom. You should maintain good posture with a form that is not considered crude or insulting like the cross-legged position in North America and places in Europe. In Asia and the Middle East it is also bad habit to point with the feet or move an object with the feet. So if you're strange and have some odd foot fetishes, you might just want to save them for behind closed doors...

The Nasals

Few of us think of the nose as being an indicator of body language, but then again, few of us consciously think of body language to begin with. In Europe the nose is involved in tapping, usually to indicate that what has occurred or what has been said is secretive or confidential. In Italy, a simple nose-tap may simply indicate the need for awareness: "look out!"

In many cultures, we blow our noses using a handkerchief or tissue. If it's a handkerchief, we then put it back in our pocket and carry it around with us. However, we typically try to hide nose-blowing because it is considered unsanitary or unbecoming. In Asia, however, this act is merely an attempt to rid the body of waste and/or toxins. It is considered healthy and nothing to hide.

Arm Movement

This may seem like a stereotype, but Italians really do use their arms in pronounced fashion to signal feelings, emotions, and attitudes. Freely moving these appendages may accentuate what is said or simply express strong feelings such as anger, happiness, and excitement. In Japan, however, the arms are typically kept stationary.

Moving them about excessively is impolite and an affront to the reserved nature of the culture.

Hand Puppets

Well maybe not hand puppets exactly, but using the hands for expression is definitely common in a variety of cultures. Firstly, hand waves are used for greeting, beckoning, or saying goodbye. The American 'goodbye' may be interpreted in Europe and Latin America as a way to say "no." On the other hand, the Italian 'goodbye' wave may signal a 'come hither' to Americans. Of course, in Asia the American 'come hither' is demeaning, as it usually pertains to summoning animals. Asians use a similar hand movement but keep the palm down.

Many of us are familiar with the handshake, but few of us realize that doing so in Asia may come across as strange. In Asian countries, a bow, prayer-like gesture, or soft handshake is preferred. Firm handshakes may be great in

Western culture, but such strong grips will come across as hostile in Asia. Furthermore, the right hand is considered more significant and the left hand desecrated in certain Asian and Middle Eastern countries. Offering or receiving gifts should be done with the right hand. When making a thumbs-up, however, it doesn't matter which hand you use. To most of us, it means good job or OK. Unfortunately, in Australia, New Zealand and African countries, the thumbs-up is a clear insult.

So watch what your hands are doing! You might just end up making yourself a new best enemy…

But more than that, watch *everything* you're doing. If you find yourself in unfamiliar territory, try to observe others around you who know what they're doing. Better yet, just know what to expect beforehand. Do the research on specific customs, get 'briefed' by others in the know, and keep yourself under control. No need to make a grand entrance; better to start soft and subtle, and pick up the cues from there.

After all, this is life we're talking about. You never know *where* you're going to end up...

Decoding Deception: How to Identify a Liar

But what happens if we end up in a situation where things just don't add up? What if a person's body signals are somehow incompatible with the feeling in our gut? What if we know what we see, but feel something vastly different?

Is the person lying? Is the person hiding something? Is the person misrepresenting the truth? And by how much? Is it but a harmless fib? Is it a moderate lie? *Or* are we bearing witness to something monumental? An act of deceit so great, that uncovering its truth could unravel the very existence of mankind as we know it....

Okay, so it's probably not *that* big of a deal, but still…

Knowing how to spot a liar is important, especially in today's world where everybody is trying to get ahead. With all the sociopaths and egomaniacs walking around out there, we better be prepared. If we know what to look for, we know what to think. And if we know what to think, we might just know how to become a master of deception ourselves.

Not that *anybody* would want to do that…

But before we do that or *this*, or anything having to do with deception, we must know one thing:

The Reference Line

This term refers to each person's unique starting point. This starting point is state of being in which the individual is unthreatened and truthful. This incorporates a given person's 'normal' speech tone, gestures, blinking patterns, movements, etc. These normal signs will differ for everybody and it is important to learn these idiosyncrasies, at least somewhat, before judging if a person is lying. After all, some body signals attributed to deception may just be natural anxiety-relievers or normal stress responses to high intensity situations. Once this reference line or baseline has been established, we can begin to determine lying on an individual basis.

That said, most people *will* exhibit common signs. Liars typically overcompensate by either making too much eye contact, or if they're unskilled at lying, they will noticeably avoid eye contact. They also make a variety of odd movements, ticks, and subtle gestures that hint at their deception. If they are trying hard to hide their lying, they may become inhumanly still. Even so, the cluster of body language most present in liars has been shown to be hand touching, face touching, leaning back, and folding the arms.

These behaviors and more are explained in detail:

Odd Response

This refers not necessarily to the response itself but to the manner in which it is delivered. Say for instance, you ask your friend if he saw an accident happen. If your friend responds extremely quickly, almost cutting you off, there is a good chance that the response was premeditated. This doesn't automatically mean it's a lie, but it does indicate that the person was wary enough to plan ahead—suggesting he or she doesn't want to be 'caught off guard' unprepared. In cases where the deceiver does not anticipate a question, he or she will exhibit the opposite behavior. This is characterized by a lag in response time, as the person scrambles to come up with a believable reply.

Flimsy Smile

Smiles aren't as easy to fake as we think. Remember, a real smile crinkles the corners of the eyes and changes the entire face. A fake smile only changes the mouth. If somebody wants you to believe he or she is happy or content, keep your eyes peeled.

Hand and Face touching

The average person touches his or her face 2,000 to 4,000 times a day. In lying persons, this touching is specific. Typically, a liar will unconsciously rub or graze the noise just prior to a lie or absurd statement. People telling fibs will also cover their mouths or rub their hands. Partially concealing the eyes is another telltale sign. This happens because the brain tells the person to 'conceal' the truth, and thus the person does so both mentally and physically.

Verbalism

Ever seen a person struggle to answer a question by not really answering the question? If you've watched a politician or two, you have. In this case, the liar may start rambling, fumbling, or employing choice words that obscure or evade a direct response. People may say things such as "as far as I know" or "I'm pretty sure" or "from what I can recall" to qualify the response. Also a liar's vocal tone will typically be higher than when somebody tells the truth. Even the use of contractions has been shown to decrease when liars are speaking. They may say, "I was *not* present at the place of murder" instead of "I *wasn't* present at the place of murder." This is believed to be an attempt to overemphasize the "not," so as to *seem* more forthcoming. Many liars, especially those with something serious to hide, are over-conscious of their responses.

Eye of the Lie

Liars typically have pupil dilation. This occurs as a result of the increase in tension and concentration required to deceive, and is almost impossible to fake. When lying, a person's blink rate will also change. Blinking will slow when the person makes the decision to lie, and will remain slow throughout the telling of said lie. However, immediately following the lie, blinking may increase dramatically.

Restless Legs

If somebody is lying, chances are his or her feet will give a sign. The anxiety caused by lying results in nervous energy that is relieved through leg folding, shifting, as well as fidgeting and shuffling of the feet. The feet or legs may also stretch, curl or even kick out as if the brain is trying to spur the body to flee. People will often ensnarl an inanimate object with their legs or feet during the telling of a lie. Look for more subtle movements as well, such as messing with shoes or scrunching toes on the carpet.

Dry Mouth

We tend to get dry in the mouth when we're nervous. Or perhaps we just become more aware of preexisting bodily discomforts. Regardless, whether you're thirsty or not to start with, telling a lie will make you reach for the water. Sometimes, deceivers will swallow in gulps, seeking instant hydration and moistening of the lips.

Body Position

This one is critical. A person being deceitful will often lean back and cross his or her arms, signifying discomfort and/or defensiveness. Typically, this is not a person who wants to be approached, and certainly not a candidate for honest and open dialogue. The person may cross the arms and lean back to 'distance' him or herself from other people, as well as to create psychic distance between his or her true intentions and his or her alleged intentions.

Gesture Change

Many liars will keep their bodies very still in order to hide any giveaways. This of course, is the biggest give away of all. If a person is rigid and unmoving, that's a good indication he or she is either doing it consciously or unconsciously is very tense. In order to appease questioners, many liars may follow up lies with gestures they believe to show passivity and submissiveness, such as rubbing hands, fidgeting with clothing accessories, messing with hair, and biting the lips. Also be on the look-out for micro-expressions, which are momentary dead giveaways to the person's true intent. They happen very fast, but are often unrealized by the liar. If she says she is happy for a new couple but you see the eyes tense with anger for a split second, trust your gut.

The Assessment Shot

This "shot" is actually a quick glance. It occurs after a lie is told and is the liar's attempt to assess the damage. The liar will typically tell the lie, look down and away, and then glance back at you to see how you've accepted the lie.

Incompatibility

In general, when body language does not match spoken words, something fishy is going on. If a person shakes his or her head, but signifies agreement through his or her words—something is amiss. Furthermore, when a person tells you he or she is feeling great while staring blankly and bleakly, that person is certainly not being completely honest. At the very least, there is internal conflict if not deceit.

Always Remember:

Body language is about clusters. No one body sign is going to tell you that a person has lied. What you need to look for are groupings of these signs occurring simultaneously or successively. Most liars will always fold arms, lean away, and touch the face and hands in some shape or form.

Again, the above signs are not surefire ways to detect liars, as some people can lie through their teeth without breaking a sweat—not to mention some people are from different cultures. But still, for decoding liars who *aren't* CIA operatives, the aforementioned signals are telling.

But enough about deceit and deception. What about using body language for other means? How about controlling your *own* body language? How about taking your meager or less-than-stellar existence and jumpstarting your life through some all-powerful, all-encompassing body talk?

That's right, I'm talking about self confidence.

And when it comes to jacking up your self-esteem, it all starts with how your body walks the walk and talks the talk…

The Science of 'Swagger': How to Master Self-Confidence and Influence Others through Body Language

Confidence is critical to life. Not only does it make us feel better about ourselves and our circumstances, it also improves the lives of others. Think about it. Who wants to be around a dejected sap with a doom-and-gloom attitude? Chances are, being around this person will only make us feel bad. If we spend *enough* time around somebody with this temperament, we may very well begin to adopt their views as our own.

Now imagine being around a powerful, beloved leader. Imagine what it is like to feed off of that energy, to feel as if the world is ripe with opportunity, as if you too can elevate your game and enjoy increased success simply with the right mindset. Being around a confident person seems to breathe new life into our world. We dream bigger, we work harder, and we live more freely.

Being confident is critical to success and happiness, and it all starts with how we present ourselves. As a matter of fact, simply changing our body language will actually trick our mind into feeling more confident. And then the cycle begins; from body to mind, mind to body.

Take a look at the following images:

Notice how the "High Power Poses" are more direct and dominant. There is nothing being hidden. The two men and the woman in the chair are leaning back, torsos exposed, laps exposed, legs at ease, arms casually resting, as if to say "here I am, I have nothing to fear." These are confident poses because they exhibit an acceptance of oneself—beyond that, a celebration of oneself. There is no insecurity. The body is saying that it is willing to show itself, regardless of how that exhibition is judged or perceived.

In the other two high power poses, a woman stands with hands on hips and hands on desk, leaning forward. In these poses, the body communicates a more dominant pose. The woman is leaning forward not backwards, showing that she is not afraid. Her hands are on the desk, a very tactile experience, indicating that she is willing to 'get the hands dirty.' Meanwhile, the woman with her hands on her hips is communicating that she doesn't care what people think. Maybe she is skeptical or mad or merely deep in consideration. No matter the emotional state attached to this pose, the pose exhibits definite body openness. The arms are exposed, the chest is exposed, the feet are pointing right ahead—the woman is not withering away from challenge.

Now look at the "Lower Pose Pose." Notice what they all have in common. They are defensive, weak, uncertain, concealed. They show a definitive insecurity present in folded arms and tilted heads and face-touching, downward-leaning, and contractive closure. Instead of confidently approaching the challenge head-on, these poses shy away from it. They say, loudly and clearly, "I'm not ready, because I'm not confident."

It may seem silly that changing your posture will make much of a difference, but the science disagrees. Studies reveal that high-power nonverbal displays cause neuroendocrine and behavioral changes for both males and females. Specifically, high-power posers show significant increases in testosterone, and decreases in cortisol, corresponding with self-reported feelings of power and risk tolerance. Low-power posers experience the opposite.

Simply put, positioning your body a certain way actually changes your chemistry for the better. Decreasing cortisol levels are good because cortisol causes stress and stress-related damage. Higher testosterone levels are also good because testosterone has been linked to improved cardiovascular health, decreased fat, increased muscle, denser bones, improved libido, and improved mood.

Standing in a power position can become a habit that affects the rest of our lives. Try sleeping on a firmer mattress (even the floor if you're daring!). If you don't want to do that, practice power positions at least a few minutes a day, preferably in the morning after you wake up. Make a conscious effort to keep your shoulders back and your head high. Work at feeling good and remember those awesome benefits. If you begin to incorporate these positions into your everyday life, you will unconsciously dictate other people's behaviors as well.

They will respect you, they will listen to you, and they will become *attracted* to you. In many cases, they might not even know why. Maybe they'll just feel your aura, and sense that you have something that they want. Regardless, the powers are incredible. Coworkers will notice a difference and approach it favorably. Friends and acquaintances will respond to you in ways they may never have. Men and women in general will see you more positively.

Here are some tips for maximizing self-confidence through the language of your body:

Preparing for the Business Meeting or Interview

Everybody wants to land that dream job. If you're sitting in a waiting room, preparing yourself mentally for an important interview, remember one thing: your sitting position.

Are you hunched over, staring at your smartphone, pondering what you're going to do and say once the secretary calls your name? Instead of sitting in the reception area with your body contracted and your eyes mostly downward, incorporate an object. Try reading a book, focusing on keeping your shoulders back and your back straight. Spread your arms out as you hold a newspaper or leaf through a book. This will ensure that your hormones are at the right level when you are finally called into the meeting. Your cortisol will be lower, your testosterone higher. As a result, you will waltz into that interview with less anxiety, more confidence, and a greater sense of self-purpose.

Defuse the Tension

Verbal fights and physical fights often stem from miscommunication. One person or both people, or multiple people, all want to be heard or acknowledged. When they aren't, or when their points are dismissed or belittled, things can become very tense very quickly. In these situations, it's best simply to realize that problems come largely from body language. If you are squared up, in somebody's face and moving closer—you're only going to exacerbate the issue. However, studies show that if you stand or position adjacently to the person with whom you're arguing, you will likely defuse the situation. This is a non-confrontation tactic that shows the person you are 'on their side,' even if your words do not. Another thing to try is to mirror the person's body movements. If overdone, this may anger him or her further—if done subtly, this will communicate a level of sympathy or empathy that might just defuse the conflict.

Take up Space

No matter where you go. Whether it's a bar, a restaurant, your workplace, a friend's house—take up space. Now, this doesn't mean that you should selfishly occupy more area than is necessary when other people clearly need somewhere to sit or stand. What this does mean, is to be assertive. Claim your territory and allow others to know it without yelling it. Don't cross your legs or tuck in your shoulders and head; be expansive instead. If you're sitting, sit larger and walk with bigger strides. Others will see you as physically bigger when you do so.

Triple-Up

This refers to a nod in which you quickly nod three times. It is a good way to communicate interest or peace. By nodding three times after a person talks, you will communicate that you understand and would like them to continue talking. This may be an effective tactic for otherwise nervous or quiet people who are not normally socially active. This will show both engagement and help to prolong a conversation. Also, if you're an introvert, it's a good way to get a person to keep talking without feeling excessive pressure to talk yourself.

Smile like a Fool

Smiling is one of those things that has been shown to have numerous benefits. This mind-over-body approach teaches us one thing: If you believe it, your body will show it. When it comes to smiling, not only does the simple act communicate positive emotions to ourselves and others, but it also gives us an extra boost of power. Studies show that smiling during difficult or stressful tasks such as exams and workouts will increase performance. This is associated with the neurochemical changes that occur when our brain tells us that everything is okay. Students perform better on assessments, and athletes have been shown to exhibit general increases in strength and endurance, such as in running, lifting weights, swimming, and the like. Not to mention, smiling shows confidence in your own skin, and allows you to influence others more readily.

Calm and Contained

Extroversion is valued in many societies because it is believed to represent the most successful approach. People who are extroverted are more outgoing, more exuberant, and more likely to form lasting social networks and use them for improvement. However, extroversion can also have its downside. When overly extroverted, especially in business meetings, interviews, or presentations, people will feel threatened. They may feel exhausted by the constant barrage of externalized energy. In cases like this, it is best to use subtlety. Try to slow down your speech, making it more concise and poignant. Limit gestures to a lesser, lower level on the body—around the waist. Always be sure to pause prior to important messages. These simply strategies will help ensure that you appear more powerful and confident.

** It should be noted that you don't have to have confident body language to influence another. It all depends on your goal. If you want somebody to feel bad for you or help you, you can easily assume a submissive pose or gesture. If you want somebody to think you're weak or incapable, only to surprise them later—you can just as easily adopt low-power poses. It's all about your agenda. Of course, this is not to say that you *should* do these things. But it is good to know them. Sometimes, we may find ourselves in situations where morals are murky and problems are tough. The road of life is never predictable. If you find yourself in a sticky situation, it is always good to have options.

And sometimes, these options lead us to places we never could have expected…

The Dangerous Game of Sexual Manipulation

Like body language, sex has its <u>own science.</u> In fact, they are both part of the *same* science. For the most part, sex and the body go together wonderfully. Limbs, heads, and slick, sweaty organs doing their thing and doing it pleasurably.

But what happens when body language and sex form a dangerous union? What happens when manipulation for the end-goal of sex becomes not merely an act, but a defining, effortless facet of a person's being?

Some people are great at manipulation. And some manipulate for the sole purpose of that carnal, pleasurable act. Others may engage as part of an exchange. Sex for shelter, sex for money, sex for a job, sex in order to give a relationship a shot. But some just want it all for themselves.

We've all experienced or seen them. At both ends of the spectrum, they are easily noticed. A hunky man with all the right words and moves; a sexy, alluring woman who has our balls in a vice without us even caring. However, you don't have to look like Brad Pitt or Angelina Jolie to use body language for sexual manipulation.

There are countless people who use body language to seduce others, to get what they want, and/or to manipulate others into compromising sexual activity. Maybe some of us have been victims, waking up the next morning next to people we regret ever meeting. Perhaps alcohol or drugs played a role, but body language certainly carried it through. Or maybe some of us have been the 'conquistadors,' waking up smiling at the fact that we got the one we wanted, if only for a night.

Let's look at some of the tactics used.

<u>BY MEN:</u>

The Come-and-Go

This one is used by men to incite a pang of jealousy in a woman of interest. Basically, the man approaches and shows that he is attracted. He offers compliments on her appearance, has steady eye contact and a confident smile. Then, just as the woman is feeling good, the man breaks away. Instantly, he finds another group of women and begins to chat it up with them. He smiles and laughs with this new group, leaving the first woman feeling as if suddenly she has to prove herself to him. Of course, sometimes this backfires and the first woman loses interest, but if executed subtly, the man will only elicit more interest from all females.

Pointing out Insecurities

Dominant males will point out a woman's flaws and insecurities. When done effectively, it makes the woman feel slightly inferior, increasing desire for a 'superior' man who can protect her. Men will employ humor as they indicate a stain on a woman's clothing, smudged makeup, worn nail polish, birthmarks, or some other superficial thing. Some men may even belittle parts of a woman's body while accentuating this remark with some form of touch, such as a butt-pinch, shoulder rub, or waist-hold.

False Implication

This is where a man uses body language in a way that leaves the woman guessing. For instance, a man might be standing off to the side, making eye contact with a woman. A second later as he approaches, the woman expects him to come up and say something. Instead, the man gently skirts by the woman, perhaps saying something softly, or not saying anything at all. A man might also touch a woman on the waist as if to signify further body contact, only to then nudge her out of the way as he continues somewhere else.

Men may also be more forward in their falsehoods, telling a woman that they will be right back, that they will call them or meet them, only to never follow through. Done repeatedly, this will often send the woman the signal that he is not interested. However, used selectively, it only intensifies desire.

Setting the Script

Men seeking to seduce women know that power is attractive. Instead of seeming wimpy or submissive like many men seeking an attractive woman, a powerful man will set the rules from the beginning. He'll let a girl know what he does and doesn't want, and will show no fear in the prospect of her leaving him. In fact, this man's lack of insecurity over being single is likely to intensify the attraction.

Work the Body

This is probably the most effective power of the sexually manipulative man. Unlike unconfident men, men with manipulative power understand the erogenous zones of the female body. They know that saying something with words is one thing; saying it with the body is the *real* thing.

When a man stimulates the right areas of a woman's body, there is little she can do. Even if she tries to resist him; even if she knows all he wants is sex.

Work the thighs

The inside of the thighs are full of nerves and love a good, stroking, kissing or licking. Fondling this area sexually excites a woman, but only once she is warmed up. Approaching too quickly and aggressively is a turn off—dominant men know this. Instead, they work it slow, gently grazing the flesh, rubbing in concentric circles, tracing the clothing line, going from rub to kiss to lick to suck, vice-versa.

Work the Feet

Dominant men know that many women love a good, sensual massage of the feet. Some women even have strange foot fetishes. Whether playing 'footsie' under the table, rubbing those freshly pedicured toes, or sucking them clean, women love a man that tends to the details.

Talented seducers can bring the woman from fringe of ticklishness to height of pleasure.

Work the Wrists

Women often show their wrists as a sign of submissiveness. But this is more than just showing deference—it is also an invitation. Dominant men know to nuzzle and nibble the woman's wrist. When used in conjunction with kissing, some women may be unable to resist!

Work the Lips

The top erogenous zone is the lips. This area provides intimate stimulation and a wide array of opportunities for further sexual activity. When a woman is kissed the right way, she not only feels desired and beautiful, but she is more likely to trust the man. It is a very personal connection, and can be made even more erotic through tongue action, slight biting, nibbling, and licking. Cunning men will often pull away, denying the woman a throaty kiss just as things get hot and heavy. This tactic will leave women breathless and hungry, wanting nothing more than to devour (and be devoured)!

Work the Butt

Women take pride in a nice behind, and men know it. This is why manipulative men know that fondling a woman's buttocks is a surefire way to get her excited. Sometimes they start with a tickle, and then progress to a rub, a caress, or a firm grab. Mild spanking and squeezing can be an especial turn-on, as can kissing, licking or sucking.

Men who want to get laid know that it all starts with initial contact. This can be seen on the dance floor, where a man will typically align himself behind a woman, giving her the freedom to move her buttocks against body in seductive fashion. By guiding her by the hips, and occasionally controlling her motions, the man gives her a taste of the kind of moves he can perform in the bedroom.

Work the Neck

The neck is very sensitive, and an easy area to exploit. By stroking the nape, the back of the neck, men can suck a woman's power right from them. Studies show that this area is highly sensitive, even to breathing. Using a little teeth can escalate the mood quickly, as can kissing and sucking beneath the chin, along the jugular. These areas are very intimate and communicate that the man is both sensual and erotic.

Work the Ears

Whispering in a woman's ear is a good way to convince them to do 'naughty.' Kissing or licking the ear is also a powerful next step that men take to work the body. This will make their spine shiver, and will likely leave women wanting more—much more.

In general, the female body is akin to a fine instrument. While some women like to jump right into it, many more will want to be gently warmed up. Manipulative men will understand this entirely, learning to subtly but assertively work towards sex. Although their intentions may be to manipulate, they will remain desirable because of their urbane ways. They will dress to highlight their goods, assume power-poses, hint at sex, use lingering touches, and eventually bring the sexual tension to the boiling point.

But men aren't the only culprits in sexual manipulation. Women are just as deceptive, if not more.

<u>Female Tactics</u>

Self-touching

Women know that men are looking at their bodies, and they know that the slightest motion, if done right, can break through to even the most stoic of men. This is why women spend a lot of time self-touching and self-modifying their appearance to draw attention. Furthermore, women have more nerve sensors than men, which makes stimulation that much more important.

At first encounter, women will use this to their advantage. They will smooth their clothes, adjust their shirts or tops, and generally groom themselves. Not only does this happen because men may make women self-conscious, it also happens because women want men to look.

Women are subtle and will come to caress and touch their bodies sensually. If a woman rubs her neck, her thigh, her arm, or her stomach, she is doing several things. Firstly, she is drawing attention to her most prominent features; secondly, she is indicating that she wants the man to touch those parts as well; and thirdly, she is stimulating herself as the interaction progresses.

Lusty Lips

Whether vaginal lips or facial lips, the plumper, the sexier. Many years ago, the Egyptians believed that women's genital lips developed in proportion to their genital lips. As it turns out, the female facial lips do become plumper during puberty. Subcutaneous fat makes them thicker and fuller, and lipstick can be thought of as an unconscious way to communicate that the woman is sexually mature— mimicking the flushing of genital lips during arousal.

But it gets even better. Every man has seen how a woman can command her lips in sultry, alluring fashion. When she starts pouting and wetting her lips in addition to lowering her eyelids, things are getting hot—and quick.

Women who really want to play with a guy will use cylindrical objects in order to suggest what they can do with their lips. They may rub the object with their thumb and index finger, a cigarette, a long earring, a straw, a long glass—and a variety of other phallic objects.

Legs & Thighs:

Where the feet point, the heart follows. The lead foot or both feet will point and indicate that the man nearby is desired. At times when one leg is tucked under another leg, the tucked under leg will angle the knee toward the man of interest.

Crossed legs also have important meaning. When used with other contractive, low-power poses, crossed legs indicate negativity, defensiveness and/or uncertainty. However, when the legs are crossed in the absence of other negative poses, the woman is trying to draw attention to her swath of flesh. The woman will typically pressure one leg firmly against the other to show muscle tone. Some psychiatrists believe this pose is an obvious prerequisite to sexual intercourse.

Face Framing

Many times, a woman will bring her hands together by placing one over the other and resting her chin on them. Although we are taught that people support their heads when bored or disinterested, this gesture means something different. It means that a woman likes the company of the man and wants to highlight her face to make it easily admired. Which is also a great way to show off her most communicative features: the eyes and lips

Hot Hair

Women take great pride in their hair, and they want men to know it. During flirtation, women will flick the hair over their shoulder or to the side. This allows the man to see their facial features and also draws attention to the hair itself. Research also shows that flipping the hair helps to disseminate perfume as well as expose the woman's arm pit, which contains the hormones known as pheromones.

Pheromones are incredibly powerful. They affect us mostly unconsciously and pull us into the worlds of infatuation, lust, and love. Pheromones are spread in a variety of ways, and hair is a great, flashy, sexy way that women do it. When a woman starts gently stroking or rubbing her hair, she is really showing it off.

Womanly Wrist

The wrists are a very fragile and delicate part of the human body. We tend to protect them without even thinking about it—every time we walk and face them inward. However, women who are signaling attraction will keep them exposed. This is alluring to men because it shows a certain submissiveness on the part of the female, as if to say, "I'm here, I'm vulnerable, I'm yours." The wrists are also highly erogenous as women have many nerve receptors there. When women are attracted and/or want to attract a man, they will show their wrists by rubbing them, opening them on a table, applying perfume to them, and revealing them when smoking.

Over-the-Shoulder

Women may choose to look at men sideways while raising their shoulder slightly upwards, signaling submissiveness, curiosity, and a certain degree of innocence. This pose also accentuates the curves of the feminine form, and is alluring to most men who find gentle, coy women to be highly attractive.

Hot Hips

Men love hips on women. Not only do they signify fertility and child-bearing ability, but the dip at the pelvis offers a great leverage point for men to express their relative dominance. Because women have a wider gap at their crotch, they are able to walk in a way that wiggles the hips and drives men crazy. Men unconsciously find women with a 70% waist-to-hip ratio most attractive, as these women are shown to have the greatest reproductive potential. Women may draw a man in by tilting those hips from side to side or putting their whole weight on one leg to make that hip side protrude. As Shakira says, the "hips don't lie!"

Except when they do…

Purse Power:

The purse is a very powerful indicator of femininity. It contains all items and products cherished by a woman, and sometimes much, much more. When it comes to the position of the purse, women will put it in a place where men can see it. If a woman wants to convey comfort with a man, she will allow him to hold her purse, fetch her purse, or may simply graze the man with the purse or touch the purse when talking to the man. Of course, a woman who doesn't feel threatened by a man may simply use him to grab her purse. If she considers him a platonic friend with no shot in hell of getting with her, allowing him into her purse may mean very little. Or maybe she wants to seduce the man by having him check into her purse and find that birth control...

It should be noted that men and women who employ the above tactics are not necessarily manipulative. Sometimes the body language happens unconsciously, because the man or woman is genuinely attracted to the other. However, certain people are less than honest. In today's world, capitalizing on body language can be the difference between going nowhere and rising to the top of your game. Whether in sex, work, or life at large, every day is an opportunity to use body language for good reason.

Unfortunately, body language is just as easily used for nefarious reasons. Some people may call this 'persuasion,' not manipulation, but the facts still stand: if we want to make the most out of body language, we can. No matter the outcome.

The Body of Work

Overall, body language is amazing. It enables us to supercharge our lives and command our networks. It allows us to venture into a new world of communication and reciprocation. In general, body language is comprised of countless interrelated parts. Facial expressions trigger muscles which elicit emotions which impact attitudes and affect behaviors. Eye contact establishes rapport or creates dissent. It makes our enemies and woos our lovers. Through gestures, we show people how we feel and think, what we want and how we want it. We form bonds, and associations; we settle disagreements, seal deals, start meetings and end projects. Through physical contact, we facilitate everything. Touching shows somebody how we feel or how we *want* them to think we feel. It is a vehicle for showing our human side; our loving side. When combined with postures and poses, touching can bring trust to a skeptic and confidence to a leery, squirrely shell of a person.

Through body language, more so than any other language, we can enact change. We can change our ways, our worlds, and the worlds of others. By consciously applying the most innate form of human communication—the form that serves the most intelligent life-forms on Earth—we can all begin the transformation.

We can transform ourselves into powerful, charismatic, self-confident parents, coworkers, friends, children, lovers and livers. We can transform our lives starting today.

And all without a single word…

***

A Special Note:

Thank you for reading "*Body Language Explained: How to Master the Power of the Unconscious.*" If you enjoyed reading this book and would like to be included on an email list for when similar content is available, feel free:

As always, thank you for reading.

And may you continue to live healthily and happily.

Sincerely,

C.K. Murray

Other works by C.K. Murray:

1. _Sex Science: 21 SIZZLING Secrets That Will Transform Your Bedroom into a Sauna_

2. _How to Help an Alcoholic: Coping with Alcoholism and Substance Abuse_

3. _The Blood Pressure Diet: 30 Recipes Proven for Lowering Blood Pressure, Losing Weight, and Controlling Hypertension_

4. _The Stress Fallacy: Why Everything You Know Is WRONG_

5. _Confidence Explained: A Quick Guide to the Powerful Effects of the Confident and Open Mind_

Made in the USA
Middletown, DE
30 December 2018